Nita Mehta's
Food for Children

Nita Mehta

B.Sc. (Home Science), M.Sc. (Food and Nutrition), Gold Medalist

SNAB

Nita Mehta's

Food for Children

ISBN 81-7869-160-4

Exclusive Distributor:

AM PRODUCTIONS
DIVISION OF: INFORMATION SCIENCE INDUSTRIES (CANADA) LIMITED

1169 Parisien St., Ottawa, Ont., K1B 4W4,
Tel: 613.745.3098 Fax: 613.745.7533
e-mail: amproductions@rogers.com
web: www.amproductions.ca

Published by:

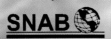

SNAB
Publishers Pvt. Ltd.
3A/3 Asaf Ali Road,
New Delhi - 110002
Tel: 23252948, 23250091
Telefax:91-11-23250091
INDIA

Editorial and Marketing office:
E-159, Greater Kailash-II, N.Delhi-48
Fax:91-11-29225218, 29229558
Tel:91-11-29214011, 29218727, 29218574
E-Mail: nitamehta@email.com, nitamehta@nitamehta.com
Website:http://www.nitamehta.com
Website: http://www.snabindia.com

Printed at:

PRESSTECH LITHO PVT LTD, NEW DELHI

Price: $ 5.95

Contents

snacks   6

complete meals   29

tiffin surprises   16

shakes & sweet delights   40

INTRODUCTION

"**M**y child will not eat anything – what shall I do?" A common complaint of exasperated mothers! This book has been written to offer children food that is different and new, to arouse their natural curiosity and adventurous spirit. Let them look at the pictures and point out what they want to eat!

Food for Children is a cookbook with a difference: the recipes were chosen by children for children; they helped to test them and it was the majority vote that decided which should be included. The result is a selection of recipes for all ages, some familiar basics that children all over the world never get tired of, and other recipes that have been specially created for this book.

You will find breakfast and lunch recipes that are easy and quick to make, recipe for tiffin-boxes, and a section on desserts that every child will adore.

Each recipe in this book has been tried and tested. All the ingredients have a good nutritive value and are easily available in your kitchen. You will find the instructions easy to follow. So relax and enjoy watching your child grow up healthy and happy and enjoying his food!

Nita Mehta

INTERNATIONAL CONVERSION GUIDE

These are not exact equivalents; they've been rounded-off to make measuring easier.

WEIGHTS & MEASURES

METRIC	IMPERIAL
15 g	½ oz
30 g	1 oz
60 g	2 oz
90 g	3 oz
125 g	4 oz (¼ lb)
155 g	5 oz
185 g	6 oz
220 g	7 oz
250 g	8 oz (½ lb)
280 g	9 oz
315 g	10 oz
345 g	11 oz
375 g	12 oz (¾ lb)
410 g	13 oz
440 g	14 oz
470 g	15 oz
500 g	16 oz (1 lb)
750 g	24 oz (1½ lb)
1 kg	30 oz (2 lb)

LIQUID MEASURES

METRIC	IMPERIAL
30 ml	1 fluid oz
60 ml	2 fluid oz
100 ml	3 fluid oz
125 ml	4 fluid oz
150 ml	5 fluid oz (¼ pint/1 gill)
190 ml	6 fluid oz
250 ml	8 fluid oz
300 ml	10 fluid oz (½ pint)
500 ml	16 fluid oz
600 ml	20 fluid oz (1 pint)
1000 ml	1¾ pints

CUPS & SPOON MEASURES

METRIC	IMPERIAL
1 ml	¼ tsp
2 ml	½ tsp
5 ml	1 tsp
15 ml	1 tbsp
60 ml	¼ cup
125 ml	½ cup
250 ml	1 cup

HELPFUL MEASURES

METRIC	IMPERIAL
3 mm	1/8 in
6 mm	¼ in
1 cm	½ in
2 cm	¾ in
2.5 cm	1 in
5 cm	2 in
6 cm	2½ in
8 cm	3 in
10 cm	4 in
13 cm	5 in
15 cm	6 in
18 cm	7 in
20 cm	8 in
23 cm	9 in
25 cm	10 in
28 cm	11 in
30 cm	12 in (1ft)

HOW TO MEASURE

When using the graduated metric measuring cups, it is important to shake the dry ingredients loosely into the required cup. Do not tap the cup on the table, or pack the ingredients into the cup unless otherwise directed. Level top of cup with a knife. When using graduated metric measuring spoons, level top of spoon with a knife. When measuring liquids in the jug, place jug on a flat surface, check for accuracy at eye level.

OVEN TEMPERATURE

These oven temperatures are only a guide. Always check the manufacturer's manual.

	°C (Celsius)	°F (Fahrenheit)	Gas Mark
Very low	120	250	1
Low	150	300	2
Moderately low	160	325	3
Moderate	180	350	4
Moderately high	190	375	5
High	200	400	6
Very high	230	450	7

Snacks

Cucumber Melts

The mashed potato topping is mixed with cheese and garnished with tomato ketchup – so tempting for a child!

Serves 8

INGREDIENTS

1 cucumber - cut into ¼" thick
slices without peeling
2 cheese slices - each slice cut into 4
tomato ketchup to dot

TOPPING
4 tbsp grated boiled potato
3 tbsp cheese spread
2 tbsp cream
¼ tsp salt and pinch of white pepper

METHOD

1   Keep 8 cucumber slices aside for use.

2   Blend all the ingredients of the topping in a mixer to a smooth paste.

3   Keep a piece of cheese slice on the cucumber.

4   Place the topping on the cheese slice. To get a heaped look place 2 dollops of it, one on top of the other.

5   Dot with tomato ketchup and serve.

Note: *You could use a piping bag to pipe out the topping on the cucumber slices.*

CHEESE BALLS

Well beaten eggs make these cheese balls so light. Correct frying makes them puffy and golden.

Serves 4

INGREDIENTS

150 ml/5 oz water (¾ cup approx.)
2 tbsp margarine
1 tsp salt
75 g/2½ oz (¾ cup) plain flour (*maida*)
2 small eggs
4 tbsp grated cheddar cheese
1-2 drops of vanilla extract, optional
¼ tsp black pepper
½ tsp mustard powder

METHOD

1 Put water, margarine and salt in a deep pan on low heat. Heat till margarine melts.

2 Remove from heat and stir in the flour. Return to heat, stir continuously till flour leaves the sides of the pan and becomes a thick ball. Remove from heat. Let it cool down.

3 Beat eggs till fluffy. Add beaten eggs gradually to the flour mixture, beating well after each addition.

4 Add grated cheese, pepper, mustard powder and extract. Beat well for 3-4 minutes.

5 Deep fry the balls carefully, after reading the tips given for frying.

Tips for frying Cheese Balls

1. Never heat the oil to smoking point.

2. The oil should not be too hot, but only medium hot when you start frying.

3. Shut off the burner after heating the oil. Then drop 8-10 balls at a time with wet fingers.

4. Switch on the burner again, continue to fry the balls on low heat until they puff up and get fully cooked from inside.

Chicken Triangles

Chicken cubes cooked in white sauce are spread over toast then grilled till golden – quick and tasty!

Serves 4

INGREDIENTS

6-8 slices bread
200 g/6 oz boneless chicken - cut into ½"
cubes
1 tbsp butter
½ cup grated cheddar cheese
mustard or tomato ketchup
½ tomato - cut into two pieces, remove
pulp and cut into tiny squares

SAUCE
2 tbsp butter
2 tbsp whole wheat flour (*atta*)
1 cup milk
¼ cup cream, optional
salt, freshly crushed peppercorns to taste
½ bell pepper - chopped finely (½ cup)

METHOD

1. Wash the chicken. Put in a micro proof bowl. Add butter and mix well. Microwave covered for 3 minutes. If you like, boil the chicken in ½ cup water for 5 minutes, till tender.

2. To prepare the sauce, melt butter in a heavy-bottomed pan. Add flour and stir for a minute. Add bell pepper. Stir for a few seconds. Remove from heat. Add milk, stirring continuously. Return to heat and cook, stirring continuously till thick. Add salt, pepper to taste. Remove from heat. Add cream. Keep the sauce aside.

3. To the sauce, add boiled chicken and half of the cheese. Check salt.

4. Spread mustard paste or tomato sauce on each slice of bread.

5. Spread the chicken mixture on the bread slices. Sprinkle some grated cheese. Sprinkle a few tomato pieces. Sprinkle crushed peppercorns.

6. Grill it in hot oven for 7-8 minutes or till slightly brown.

Paper Thin Veggie Chips

All kinds of root vegetables may be finely sliced and deep-fried to make 'chips'. Serve as an accompaniment to a meal or simply by themselves as a nibble.

Serves 4

INGREDIENTS

2 carrots
1 beetroot
1 sweet potato or potato
3-4 tbsp cornstarch
oil for deep frying
¼ tsp pepper
½ tsp oregano, 1 tsp salt

METHOD

1 Peel all the vegetables, then slice the carrot, beetroot and sweet potato with the help of vegetable peeler into thin long slices. Pat all the vegetables dry on kitchen paper.

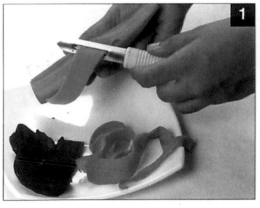

2 Heat oil in a wok. Sprinkle veggies with cornstarch and mix gently. This absorbs only excess moisture. Add the vegetable slices in batches and deep-fry for 2-3 minutes on medium heat, until golden & crisp. Remove and drain on kitchen towel.

3 Immediately sprinkle pepper, oregano and salt over the hot chips.

4 Pile up the vegetable 'chips' on a serving plate & serve immediately.

Note: *You can also make fritters (pakoras) with these vegetable slices. Dip them in a gramflour batter and deep fry to get healthy pakora chips.*

Almond French Toasts

Powdered almonds and grated cheese enrich the nutrition value and the texture of this standard breakfast favourite – French toast.

Serves 2

INGREDIENTS

4 bread slices
2 eggs
4 tbsp grated cheddar cheese
2 tbsp almond powder, see note
¼ cup finely chopped cabbage
½ tsp salt, ¼ tsp pepper
chilli powder to taste
2 tbsp milk
oil for shallow frying

METHOD

1   Whisk the eggs and add cheese, almond powder, cabbage, salt, pepper and chilli powder. Add milk.

2   Heat 2 tbsp oil in a non stick skillet or pan.

3   Dip the slices in the egg mixture. After a few seconds, turn side. Drop the slices into the hot oil.

4   Cook till the egg mixture sets. Turn the slice. Fry till brown & crisp.

5   Repeat with all the other slices. Serve whole or cut each into triangles.

Note: *Almonds can be ground and stored in a bottle. When added to recipes, they enhance the nutritive value to a great extent.*

Chicken and Corn Crostini

A long loaf of French bread is sliced to make small, thick toasts called crostini – cover them with the kids' favourite toppings and bake.

Serves 6-8

INGREDIENTS

½ loaf French bread - cut into ½" thick slices
2 tsp minced garlic
200 g/6 oz boneless chicken - cut into small pieces
½ tsp salt, ½ tsp pepper, ¼ tsp oregano
2 tbsp oil
1 tomato - pureed in the mixer (½ cup)
some chilli flakes to sprinkle
2 tbsp corn, canned or frozen

GARLIC BUTTER
3 tbsp softened butter
½ tsp minced garlic - crushed
a pinch of salt & ¼ tsp freshly crushed pepper

TOPPING
½ cup grated cheese, preferably parmesan or mozzarella
2 tbsp olive oil or melted butter

METHOD

1 Heat oil. Reduce heat. Add garlic and chicken. Stir-fry for 2 minutes or till chicken changes colour. Add salt, pepper, oregano and tomato puree. Cook covered for about 5 minutes or till chicken is tender and dry. Add corn and mix well. Remove from heat.

2 Prepare garlic butter by mixing softened butter with garlic, salt and pepper.

3 Cut French loaf diagonally into ½" thick slices. On each slice spread some garlic butter. Sprinkle some chilli flakes.

4 Arrange some chicken mixture on it. Cover with grated cheese. Spoon a little olive oil or melted butter on top of the cheese.

5 Bake in a preheated oven at 180°C/ 350°F for 10 minutes or till the base of the bread turns crisp and the cheese melts. Serve hot.

Savoury Lollipops

A mix of vegetables, breadcrumbs and chickpea paste is presented in a kid-friendly shape – irresistible for a child!

Makes 8

INGREDIENTS

6 ice cream sticks or wooden spoons
1 cup canned chickpeas/garbanzo/kabuli
channa (boiled *channas*)
½ cup boiled and mashed potato
½ cup chopped spinach
½ cup grated carrot
2 slices of bread
2 tbsp tomato ketchup
1¼ tsp salt, or to taste
½ tsp pepper powder or to taste

METHOD

1 Break bread into pieces and put in a mixer. Grind to get fresh bread crumbs. Remove from mixer.

2 Put the chickpeas/garbanzo/kabuli channa in the same mixer and grind to a paste.

3 Mix boiled and mashed potatoes with chopped spinach, grated carrots, bread crumbs, ketchup, salt and pepper. Add chick pea paste also. Mix well.

4 Make balls and insert a stick in each.

5 Flatten the ball on the stick.

6 Shallow-fry in a non stick skillet along with the stick in hot oil till golden.

Chicken Mince Satay

These elegant satay sticks will bring the grown-ups to the kids' table.

Makes 10-12

INGREDIENTS

250 g/8 oz ground chicken (mince)
½ egg
1 tsp minced garlic
½ cup finely chopped bell pepper
2 tbsp finely chopped onion
¾ tsp salt, ¼ tsp pepper, ¼ tsp oregano

OTHER INGREDIENTS

2-3 tbsp cornstarch for coating
4 tbsp oil for shallow frying
some satay sticks or bamboo skewers

METHOD

1 Put the ground meat in a strainer. Wash well and then press to drain out all the water. Leave in the strainer for 10 minutes so that all the water drips.

2 Add egg, garlic, bell pepper, onion and seasonings to the mince.

3 Make small balls. Flatten a ball on a satay stick. Do not make the satay too broad.

4 Sprinkle some cornstarch on a plate. Press satay on it to coat. Turn to coat both sides.

5 Heat 4 tbsp oil in a non stick skillet. Pan fry 5-6 satays changing sides in between, till golden and cooked. Let them be in the pan for 5-6 minutes while frying so that they get cooked well.

6 Serve with mustard or tomato sauce.

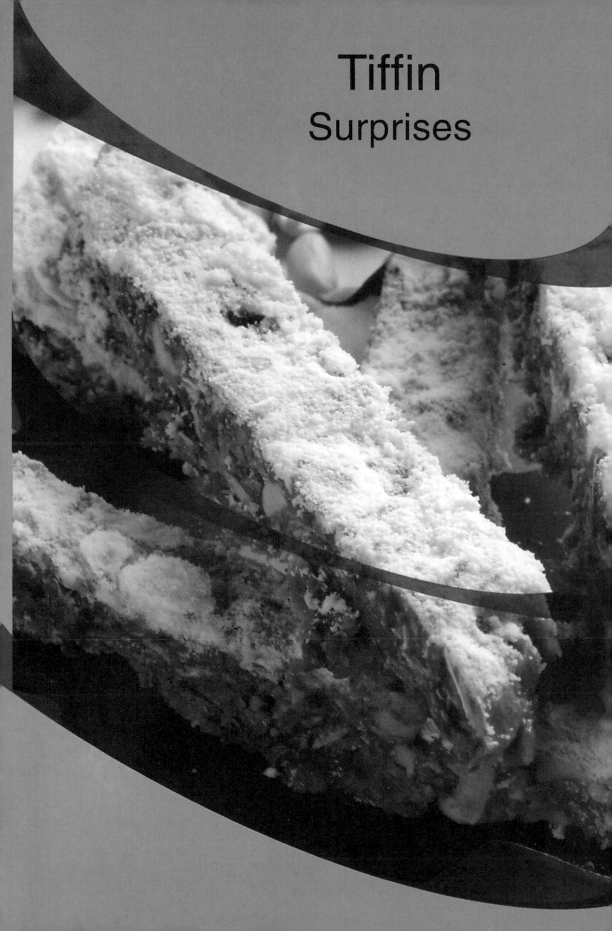

Tiffin
Surprises

Sprouty Peanut Tomato Rice

Crunchy peanuts, sprouts and veggies make this tomato-rice a hearty, happy meal.

Serves 2

INGREDIENTS

½ cup rice - soaked for ½ hour
3 tbsp peanuts
½ small onion - sliced
½ cup moong bean sprouts
1 carrot - very finely chopped (½ cup)
½ cup finely chopped green beans
2 tbsp oil
½ tsp cumin seeds (*jeera*)
2 tbsp ready-made tomato puree or
1 tomato - pureed in a mixer
½ tsp garlic paste (2-3 flakes of garlic -
crushed to a paste)
1 tsp lemon juice
¼ tsp pepper
1 tsp salt, or to taste

METHOD

1 Heat 2 tbsp oil in a heavy-bottomed pan. Add peanuts. Fry till they start to change colour. Immediately take them out of the pan and keep aside.

2 Reduce flame. Add cumin seeds, when they turn golden, add the onions. Stir-fry till light brown. Add garlic paste.

3 Add the sprouts & cook for 1 minute. Add carrot and green beans. Cook for about 2 minutes on low heat.

4 Add tomato puree, salt and pepper. Cook till the mixture is dry.

5 Drain the soaked rice. Add rice to the vegetables and stir gently for 1-2 minutes.

6 Add 1 cup water, bring to a boil. Reduce heat. Cover with a well fitting lid. Cook on very low heat till done for about 12-15 minutes.

7 When the rice is done, add the fried peanuts and lemon juice, mix lightly with a fork. Serve hot with yogurt.

Egg Rolls

Golden and crisp finger-food for hungry children!

Makes 8

INGREDIENTS

4 hard- boiled eggs
¼ cup finely chopped onion
2 tbsp very finely sliced green beans
4 tbsp grated cheddar cheese
2 tbsp cornstarch
2 slices bread - ground in a mixer to get
1 cup fresh bread crumbs
½ tsp salt, ½ tsp pepper
½ tsp prepared mustard or 1 tsp
mustard powder, 2 tsp tomato ketchup
oil for frying

METHOD

1 Grate the boiled eggs, add onion, green beans, cheese, cornstarch, salt, pepper, ketchup and mustard. Add bread crumbs.

2 Mix well. Shape into oblong rolls. Keep aside.

3 Heat oil in a pan and fry rolls, few at a time, on medium heat, till the rolls turn golden brown. Drain on absorbent paper.

Noodle Hearts

The familiar taste of maggie noodles; a new shape that grabs attention; the goodness of almonds – this snack comes First in class!

Serves 4

METHOD

1 Boil maggie noodles in just 1 cup water on medium flame till the water gets absorbed.

2 Melt butter in a heavy-bottomed pan on low heat.

3 Add flour and stir fry for 1 minute. Remove from heat & cool. Add milk stirring continuously. Return to heat.

4 Add carrots, cabbage, almond powder & cook till thick. Add salt.

5 Add boiled noodles. Cook for 2-3 minutes more & keep mixing the noodles gently. Do not mash the noodles.

6 Cook till the mixture turns thick enough to be shaped into cutlets. Remove from heat. Cool.

7 With oiled hands, make heart shaped cutlets & refrigerate overnight. Next morning shallow or deep fry.

INGREDIENTS

1 pack (100 g/4 oz) noodles (Ramen or Maggie)
2 tbsp butter
2 tbsp whole wheat flour (*atta*)
¾ cup milk
1 carrot - grated (¾ cup)
¾ cup finely chopped cabbage
1 tbsp almond powder (8-10 almonds, ground)
salt and pepper to taste

Chicken Croquettes

These mouth-watering croquettes, filled with chicken, corn and cheese have a crunchy golden crust.

Makes 16

INGREDIENTS

MICROWAVE TOGETHER
500 g/ 1 lb chicken with bones
2 tbsp oil
½ tsp salt, ½ tsp pepper, ¾ cup water

OTHER INGREDIENTS
2 tbsp butter, 2 tbsp oil
6 tbsp whole wheat flour
½ tsp crushed garlic
½ cup chopped onions, ½ cup milk
1 tbsp finely chopped parsley
½ tsp salt, ½ tsp white pepper
½ tsp red chilli flakes (or to taste)
4 tbsp grated cheddar cheese
2-3 tbsp corn
1 bread slice - ground in a mixer to get
fresh crumbs (½ cup)

COATING INGREDIENTS
1 egg white mixed with 1 tbsp water
4 tbsp cornstarch
3 bread slices - ground in a mixer to get
fresh crumbs, ½ tsp salt
2 tbsp finely chopped parsley

METHOD

1. Put chicken with oil, salt, pepper and water in a bowl. Cover with cling film and microwave for 6 minutes. Shred the chicken finely, discarding the bones. Keep stock/liquid aside.

2. Heat oil and butter in a pan. Add flour and stir on low heat for ½ minute. Add garlic and onions. Saute for 2 minutes.

3. Add the reserved stock and milk. Stir till thick and it leaves the sides of the pan. Remove from heat.

4. Add chicken, corn, parsley, salt, white pepper, red chilli flakes & cheese. Add ½ cup fresh bread crumbs. Mix lightly. Check seasonings. Cool. Shape into rolls.

5. For coating, mix bread crumbs with salt and parsley.

6. Roll a croquette over cornstarch spread on a plate. Dust off excess. Dip in egg-wash. Again roll over cornstarch and then dip in egg wash.

7. Finally roll in seasoned bread crumbs. Keep in fridge till serving time. To fry, heat oil on medium heat. Fry 2-3 at a time till golden. Drain on a paper towels. Serve with any dip or ketchup.

Suppli

Deep-fried balls made from saffron rice, with a cube of cheese in the centre – tell your child about their country of origin: Italy.

Gives 12 *large balls*

INGREDIENTS

4 tbsp butter
1 onion - finely chopped
1 cup rice
a few strands of saffron
1 tsp salt
1 tsp pepper
2 tbsp chopped fresh parsley or
coriander/cilantro
1 tbsp grated cheese (parmesan or
mozzarella)
2 eggs
75 g/2½ oz mozzarella cheese - cut into
¼" cubes
dry bread crumbs to coat

METHOD

1 Heat 2 tbsp butter. Add chopped onion. Fry for 1-2 minutes.

2 Add washed rice. Fry for 1-2 minutes.

3 Add saffron, salt and pepper.

4 Add 2½ cups water. Boil. Cover & cook on low heat till all the water is absorbed & rice is cooked. Cook further for 2 more minutes & dry the rice completely. Remove from heat.

5 Add parsley/coriander/cilantro, 2 tbsp butter & 1 tbsp grated cheese. Mix & let the mixture cool completely.

6 Beat eggs lightly and mix carefully with the cooled rice.

7 Cut mozzarella cheese into small cubes or grate it.

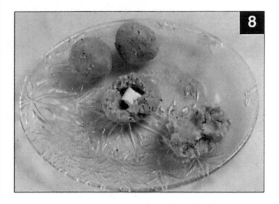

8 Divide the rice mixture into 12 equal portions. Make a ball with one portion. Flatten it. Place some grated cheese or 1-2 cubes of cheese inside and cover completely with rice mixture. Shape into a large round or oblong balls, like the shape of an egg.

9 Roll over dry bread crumbs and keep aside in the refrigerator. Do with all the rice mixture.

10 At serving time, deep fry to a golden brown colour. Serve hot.

Variation:

- A small piece of ham can be added along with the grated or cubed cheese for ham suppli.

- Left over rice or risotto can be used to make suppli.

- Can have plain suppli by omitting the saffron.

Ham & Cheese Dream

A hearty sandwich for active, growing children – serve it plain or grilled.

Serves 4-6

INGREDIENTS

8 slices bread
4 slices cheese, 4 slices ham
2-3 tsp mustard paste or pizza topping
2 tbsp butter, or enough to butter the slices

METHOD

1 Butter bread slices on one side.

2 Place a slice of cheese on the unbuttered side, keeping the buttered side outside.

3 Spread a little mustard paste or pizza topping on the cheese. Cover the cheese slice with a ham slice & place another bread slice over the ham slice with the buttered side outside.

4 Repeat this with the other slices to get 4 sandwiches.

5 Put the sandwich under a grill for 5 minutes. Turn side and brown the other side also. Cut diagonally and serve hot.

Cheese-Raisin Sandwiches

Children love these sandwiches and so do the adults!

Serves 4

INGREDIENTS

8 slices brown bread - lightly buttered
4 tbsp raisins (*kishmish*) - soak in warm water
¾ cup grated cheddar cheese
3 tbsp milk
3 tbsp mayonnaise

METHOD

1 Strain the raisins soaked in water.

2 Mix the grated cheese with milk and mayonnaise. Add raisins.

3 Butter all the slices lightly. Spread some cheese-raisin mixture on a slice and cover with another slice.

4 Trim sides. Cut into two and serve.

Note: You may reduce the amount of raisins (*kishmish*) for adults.

Peanut Butter Muesli Squares

These delectable nutritious squares are set in the fridge – no baking required!

Makes 15 squares

INGREDIENTS

½ cup desiccated coconut
200 g/7 oz sweetened condensed milk
200 g/7 oz toasted muesli (2½ cups)
35 g/1 oz peanut butter (2 tbsp)
30 g/1 oz salted butter (2 tbsp)
35 g/1 oz roasted peanuts ((2 tbsp)
80 g/3 oz icing sugar (¾ cup)
30 ml/1 oz honey (2 tbsp)

METHOD

1 Line a small loaf or rectangular dish with aluminium foil. Grease it lightly. Spread ¼ cup desiccated coconut evenly over base of tin.

2 Combine all ingredients except remaining ¼ cup of desiccated coconut.

3 Stir over low heat for about 10 minutes or till thick. Spread over coconut in the tin.

4 Sprinkle remaining coconut on top & press gently. Cover & refrigerate till firm. Cut into squares and serve.

Cheesy Pita Wedges

Who can resist these crisp, thin wedges generously buttered with garlic and cheese –
watch out kids, the grown-ups have their eyes on your plate!

Makes 16 wedges

INGREDIENTS

1 whole wheat pita bread or 1 pizza base
6 tbsp melted butter
2 flakes of garlic - crushed (½ tsp)
3 tbsp chopped fresh basil
1 tsp oregano
a pinch of salt & pepper
½ cup grated mozzarella or pizza cheese

METHOD

1 Slit pita bread/pizza base horizontally to get 2 thin rounds.

2 Cut each pita bread/pizza base round equally into 8 wedges (triangular pieces). This way you have 16 pieces in all.

3 Combine butter, garlic, basil, oregano, salt and pepper, brush over inner/cut side of bread wedges, then sprinkle with mozzarella cheese.

4 Place in single layer on oven trays.

5 Bake in a hot oven for 5-6 minutes at 200°C or until crisp.

Complete Meals

Broccoli Mayo Wraps

What a satisfying feeling to bite into a well-filled, well-flavoured wrap! For smaller hands, cut the wrap into smaller pieces.

Serves 4

INGREDIENTS

4 whole wheat tortillas

FILLING FOR 4 WRAPS
3 tbsp oil
1 tsp cumin seeds (*jeera*)
1 tsp finely chopped garlic
½ onion - cut into rings
2 cups small broccoli florets
½ cup shredded cabbage
1 tomato - chopped, 1 tbsp lemon juice
¼ tsp pepper, 1 tsp salt, or to taste

OTHER INGREDIENTS
3-4 tbsp ready-made mayonnaise or
mustard sauce
2 tbsp tomato ketchup

METHOD

1 Heat oil for filling. Add cumin and garlic. Wait till garlic changes colour. Add onion rings and stir till soft. Add broccoli and stir fry for 2-3 minutes.

2 Add cabbage and tomato, stir for 2 minutes.

3 Add lemon juice, pepper and salt to taste. Cover and cook till broccoli gets done, remove from heat.

4 Spread some mayonnaise on each tortilla, covering till the sides. Keep some broccoli mixture on it at one end. Roll up tightly. Seal the other end with some tomato ketchup.

5 To serve, heat 1 tbsp oil and pan-fry the wrap with the tucked side down till golden on both sides.

CREAMY VEGETABLE PASTA

Whole wheat pasta is a complex carbohydrate which keeps the child feeling full for a long time. Bite-size vegetables give the dish a lively look.

Watch these hungry mouths slurp the velvety red sauce full of cheese and cream!

Serves 2

INGREDIENTS

1 cup whole wheat pasta or any other pasta of your choice, 1 tsp olive oil
2 tbsp oil
1 tsp minced garlic
½ onion - chopped (½ cup)
½ cup chopped mixed vegetables (cauliflower, carrot, bell pepper, zucchini, beans or peas)
4 tbsp ready-made tomato puree
2 tsp sugar
salt and pepper to taste

CREAMY MIXTURE
¼ cup cream
2 tbsp cheese spread
3 tbsp milk

METHOD

1. Boil 6 cups water with 1 tsp oil and 1 tsp salt. Add pasta to boiling water. Boil for 8-10 minutes till pasta turns soft. Remove from heat and strain. Sprinkle 1 tsp olive oil on the pasta and keep aside in the strainer for the water to drip off.

2. Heat oil in a frying pan, add garlic and onions and cook for ½ minute.

3. Add cauliflower, zucchini, peas/beans and carrot. Cook for 4-5 minutes or till vegetables are tender.

4. Add boiled pasta. Cook for ½ minute.

5. Add tomato puree and sugar. Cook for a minute. Keep aside till serving time.

6. At serving time, mix cream, cheese spread and milk together in a bowl. Stir into the pasta, cook for about 2 minutes. The cream sauce would thicken and coat the pasta. Check salt. Serve hot with garlic bread.

Note: *If you want white pasta sauce omit the tomato puree and sugar.*

Chicken Burritos

Today's savvy youngsters are ready for adventure – treat them to Mexican burritos filled with marinated, sautéed chicken.

Serves 4-6

INGREDIENTS

4-6 whole wheat tortillas
salsa to serve

FILLING
500 g/1 lb boneless chicken - cut into thin long strips
2 tbsp Worcestershire sauce
1 tbsp soya sauce, 1 tbsp vinegar
¼ tsp red chilli flakes or red chilli paste
½ tsp salt
3 tbsp oil
1 tsp minced garlic
1 green onion - chopped diagonally including the greens
1 small green bell pepper - cut into strips (½ cup)

SOUR CREAM
½ cup cream
1 tsp lemon juice
1½ cups yogurt - hang for ½ hour in a cheese cloth
salt and white pepper to taste

METHOD

1 For the filling, marinate the chicken with Worcestershire sauce, soya sauce, vinegar and chilli paste or flakes and salt for ½ hour.

2 Heat 3 tbsp oil in a non-stick skillet. Add garlic, stir. Add the marinated chicken, cook on medium heat for 1 minute. Reduce heat. Cover and cook till chicken is tender. Add the bell pepper and green onion. Stir. Check salt and add to taste. Remove from heat.

3 For the sour cream, beat cream till stiff. Beat hung yogurt till smooth. Add cream to the yogurt. Stir in salt, pepper and lemon juice. Keep in the refrigerator.

4 At the time of serving, heat 1 tbsp oil in a skillet. Warm the tortilla in it . Remove from heat. Spread hot chicken filling at one end. Spoon 1 tbsp of sour cream over the filling. Put a few drops of salsa on it. Roll the tortilla.

5 Serve warm with left over sour cream and salsa.

GREEK MEAT POCKETS

A pocket of bread: the outside tastes like pizza, the inside holds the food – a surprise package for the children!

Serves 8

INGREDIENTS

2 thick pizza bases
4 cooked sausages - thinly sliced diagonally
1 cup corn - tinned
2 tbsp butter
1 bell pepper, green or coloured - cut into strips
½ cup shredded cabbage
2-3 tbsp tomato puree
salt & pepper to taste
some lettuce to garnish

TOPPING

1 tbsp butter
1 cup grated pizza cheese (mozzarella)
½ tsp red chilli flakes
1 tsp dried oregano

METHOD

1   Cut the pizza base into half. Slit open the cut side with the tip of a knife to make a deep pocket without damaging the top, bottom or sides of the base.

2   Push a small lettuce leaf into the pocket if you wish. Keep aside.

3   Heat butter in a non stick pan. Add cabbage and bell pepper. Saute for ½ minute. Add the sausages. Stir fry for a minute. Add the corn, tomato puree, pepper, pinch of salt and cook till puree dries and coats the sausages. Remove from heat.

4   Fill the pizza pockets with the sausage mixture, carefully without damaging the pizza.

5   Slightly butter the top of the pizza and sprinkle grated cheese, chilli flakes and oregano on top of the pizza base.

6   Heat oven to 200°C/400°F. Place the stuffed pizza on a greased grill rack for 5-7 minutes till the cheese on top melts.

7   Cut each half in 2 pieces to get 4 pieces. Serve hot.

Vegetable Train

Kids go crazy over an edible choo-choo train! Use only one kind of vegetable or use different combinations of hollowed-out veggies and fillings as suggested in this recipe.

Serves 8

1 LARGE POTATO - BOILED
½ cup chopped spinach
1 tbsp grated cheese
1 tbsp chopped onion
salt & pepper to taste, 1 tsp butter

1 Peel boiled potato. Cut a thin slice lengthways. Scoop potato leaving ½" thick wall.

2 Heat butter in a pan & add onions. Cook till soft. Add spinach. Cook for another 3-4 minutes. Add salt and pepper. Remove from heat.

3 Add cheddar cheese. Fill this mixture in the potato and keep aside.

3" PIECE ZUCCHINI
¼ onion - chopped
¼ tomato - chopped, salt & pepper
1 tsp olive oil, 1 tbsp grated cheese

1 Scoop out pulp of the zucchini piece, leaving ¼" thick wall all around. Reserve the pulp.

2 Heat 1 tsp olive oil in a pan. Saute the onion. Add tomatoes and stir for a minute. Add the pulp of zucchini. Add salt and pepper to taste. Stir fry for 3-4 minutes till cooked. Fill this mixture in the zucchini and sprinkle cheese on top. Keep aside.

3" PIECE TOFU (200 G/6 OZ)
1 tbsp coriander/cilantro - chopped
1 tbsp onions chopped, 1 tbsp tomatoes
1 tsp butter, salt & pepper - to taste

1 Scoop out tofu leaving ½" thick wall around. Keep aside.

2 Heat a pan & put butter in it. Pan fry the block of tofu & keep aside.

3 In the same pan, put onions and cook till soft. Add tomatoes, coriander, salt and pepper and stir for 1 minute.

4 Add crumbled tofu which was scooped out and stir for a minute. Remove from heat. Fill this mixture into the tofu block.

TO ASSEMBLE THE TRAIN
2 tbsp butter, 1 green onion (green part)
3 bamboo skewers, tooth picks, grapes

1 Take 2 tbsp of butter & melt it. Brush potato and zucchini nicely with melted butter. Place the vegetables on a wire rack & grill them for 10-15 minutes or until cooked.

2 Take 2 bamboo skewers and break each into 2 pieces. Insert the skewers in the green part of green onions and join the vegetables and tofu behind each other with the help of these sticks. Make wheels with black grapes inserted with toothpicks. Serve warm.

Shakes & Sweet
Delights

Spinach & Beetroot Cookies

Natural vegetable colours for these fun cookies!

Makes 30

INGREDIENTS

100 g/3 oz butter
50 g/2 oz powdered sugar
100 g/ 3 oz plain flour
2 tbsp raw spinach puree
or
2 tbsp raw beetroot puree

METHOD

1 Cream butter and sugar until very light and fluffy with an electric beater.

2 Add spinach or beetroot puree to the above mixture and beat well.

3 Add flour gradually to the mixture and mix well with a spoon to get a soft dough consistency.

4 Line a cookie sheet with aluminium foil. Grease the foil. Fill the cookie mixture in the piping bag. Pipe the desired shape.

5 Bake in a preheated oven at 200°C/ 400°F for 10 minutes. Let it cool down in the oven for 15 minutes to become crisp. Serve.

Note: *To make spinach puree, grind about ½ cup chopped spinach in a mixer to a puree. Similarly puree peeled and grated beetroot in a mixer.*

Vegetable Rainbow Cake

Can't get the kids to eat vegetables? How about putting the veggies into a cake – this striped cake receives a high five!

Serves 8

INGREDIENTS

4 eggs
150 g/5 oz butter
150 g/5 oz powdered sugar
150 g/5 oz whole wheat flour (*atta*)
1½ tsp baking powder
1½ tsp vanilla extract
1 cup chopped spinach - puree in a mixer
1 cup grated yellow pumpkin - grate & puree in a mixer
a drop of yellow food colour, optional
1 small beetroot - grate & puree in a mixer
1½ tbsp cocoa powder

METHOD

1 Sift flour and baking powder. Keep aside.

2 Beat eggs till fluffy. Keep aside.

3 Beat powdered sugar and butter till creamy. Add essence.

4 Add flour and eggs in batches to the butter-sugar mixture. Fold with a spoon.

5 Divide the mixture into 4 parts. Put about 2 tbsp of spinach puree in one part, about 2 tbsp of pumpkin puree and a drop of yellow colour to the second part and add about 2 tbsp of beetroot puree to the third part. Add enough puree to all portions to get a soft dropping consistency. Put cocoa powder to the fourth part. Add 1 tbsp milk if the batter appears too thick.

6 Grease a large loaf tin and put layers of each batter one on top of the other. Do not mix.

7 Bake in a preheated oven for about 35-40 minutes at 180°C/350°F.

8 Test by inserting a knife in the centre of the cake. If it comes out clean, remove cake from oven. Remove cake from the tin after 5-7 minutes.

Date Fingers

Mashed dates and crushed biscuits rolled in snowy-white coconut are transformed into a festive treat!

Makes 7-8 fingers

METHOD

1 Boil the dates with milk. Cook covered on low heat for about 8-10 minutes till almost dry and becomes a soft paste. Keep mashing in between.

2 In a bowl mix biscuits, 2 tbsp desiccated coconut and essence.

3 Add the cooked dates into the mix and knead to form a dough.

4 Make a 3"x5" block of ¾" thickness on a flat surface. Neaten the edges.

5 Cut into ½" broad fingers. Coat the fingers with the remaining desiccated coconut, covering all the sides completely. Serve.

Banana Berry Shake

A sweet and delicious yogurt smoothy!

Makes 1 large glass

INGREDIENTS

½ cup cold milk
½ cup chopped strawberries (3-4)
½ cup chilled yogurt
½ very ripe banana - peeled & chopped
1 tbsp strawberry crush (optional)
3 ice cubes
1 tbsp sugar

METHOD

1 Put banana, strawberries and yogurt together in the freezer for 20-30 minutes before blending the shake

2 In a mixer blend all the ingredients until smooth & serve immediately.

Apricot Almond Delight

The delicate flavour and interesting texture of juicy apricots and almonds complement each other beautifully in this light and fluffy drink.

Serves 2

INGREDIENTS

10 pieces of dried apricots
1 cup milk, 1½ tbsp sugar
½ tsp sweet almond or vanilla extract
½ tbsp finely chopped almonds

METHOD

1 Place apricots in a bowl, pour in sufficient water to cover and leave to soak for at least 3-4 hours or overnight.

2 Drain apricots and chop. Place in a food processor or blender with milk, sugar and almond essence. Process until smooth.

3 Pour into individual glasses. Refrigerate until firm.

4 To serve sprinkle with chopped almonds.

GLOSSARY OF NAMES/TERMS

Al dente Pasta and vegetables should be cooked to a texture that is not too soft; it should be 'firm to bite' which in Italian is 'al dente'.

Basil A fragrant herb

Baste To brush food with fat to prevent it from drying out.

Bean Curd See tofu

Blanch To remove skin by dipping into hot water for a couple of minutes. e.g. to blanch tomatoes or almonds.

Blend To combine two or more ingredients.

Bell Pepper Capsicum

Castar sugar Finely granulated sugar

Cheddar cheese A mature processed cheese with a lot of flavour

Cilantro See coriander

Coriander, fresh A green herb. All parts of the plant are flavourful and hence edible - leaves, stalks and the Thai also use the root of coriander. Also called cilantro in the west.

Cornflour Cornstarch

Dice To cut into small neat cubes.

Dough A mixture of flour, liquid etc., kneaded together into a stiff paste or roll.

Drain To remove liquid from food.

Garnish To decorate.

Green Onion Spring onions, scallions

Green Beans Also called French beans. The tender variety should be used.

Juliennes To cut into thin long pieces, like match sticks.

Marinate To soak food in a mixture for some time so that the flavour of the mixture penetrates into the food.

Mozarella Cheese A melting and stringy cheese

Paneer The Indian cheese prepared from milk.

Plain Flour All purpose flour, *maida*.

Powdered Sugar Icing sugar

Red Chilli Powder Cayenne pepper

Rind The outer skin of citrous fruits like lemon, orange etc.

Saute To toss and make light brown in shallow fat.

Shred To cut into thin, long pieces.

Sift To pass dry ingredients through a fine sieve.

Star Anise A star-shaped, fennel-flavoured fruit, dried and used as a spice.

Tofu Cheese prepared from soya bean milk. Also called bean curd.

Turmeric A yellow spice with antiseptic properties. Usually available as a powder. It imparts a yellow colour to food.

Toss To lightly mix ingredients without mashing them e.g. salads.